A Celebration of the Civil Rights Movement ™

THE CIVIL RIGHTS ACT OF 1964

Jennifer Bringle

ROSEN PUBLISHING®
New York

Published in 2015 by The Rosen Publishing Group, Inc.
29 East 21st Street, New York, NY 10010

First Edition

Library of Congress Cataloging-in-Publication Data

Bringle, Jennifer, author.
The Civil Rights Act of 1964/Jennifer Bringle.
pages cm.—(A celebration of the civil rights movement)
Includes bibliographical references and index.
ISBN 978-1-4777-7739-8 (library bound)
1. United States. Civil Rights Act of 1964—History—Juvenile literature.
2. Civil rights movement—United States—History—20th century—Juvenile literature. I. Title.
KF4750.B73 2015
342.7308'5—dc23

2013046691

Manufactured in the United States of America

CONTENTS

INTRODUCTION

During the late 1950s and early 1960s, the United States was at a crossroads. Across the nation, and especially in the South, African Americans faced daily discrimination and, in some cases, violence from whites who did not want them to have equal rights.

Peaceful protests against this discrimination led by civil rights activists such as Dr. Martin Luther King Jr. and organizations such as the NAACP cropped up throughout the South. The Montgomery Bus Boycott, lunch counter sit-ins, Freedom Rides, and the March on Washington gave African Americans and their allies a way to peacefully make their voices heard. And many times, these nonviolent demonstrations were met with violence. Even innocent people, such as four young girls killed in a church bombing in Birmingham, Alabama, were subjected to horrific violence.

Many Americans were shocked by the terrible things happening in the South. Among them was President John F. Kennedy,

Civil rights activist Dr. Martin Luther King Jr. joined President Lyndon B. Johnson as he signed the Civil Rights Act of 1964 into law.

who, in the summer of 1963, decided it was time to act. He proposed civil rights legislation that would make history and bring equality to millions of Americans.

In 1964, after more than a century of struggling for freedom and equal rights under the law, African Americans scored a major victory when the U.S. Congress passed the Civil Rights Act of 1964.

The landmark legislation outlawed discrimination based on race, ethnicity, nationality, or gender. It made racial segregation and other Jim Crow laws designed to prevent African Americans from voting illegal.

While this legislation was a huge step forward in the quest for freedom and equal rights for all in the United States, it wasn't the end of the fight for equal rights. The act opened the door for additional legislation that expanded civil rights for African Americans as well as other groups, such as disabled Americans and women.

The passing of the Civil Rights Act of 1964 was the result of a hard-fought battle years in the making. From the emancipation of slaves following the Civil War to early legislation during Reconstruction and the turbulent years of the civil rights movement, the struggle for equal rights is a long one.

And though the Civil Rights Act of 1964 wasn't the final battle in the fight for equal rights, it was still one of the most important moments in the process of bringing equality to all in the United States. It helped change the cultural climate of the nation and opened the eyes of many Americans to the issue of discrimination in this country. Even today, more than fifty years since the act was passed, its legacy of freedom, equality, and justice lives on.

Chapter 1

A HISTORY OF INEQUALITY

At the height of the Civil War in 1863, President Abraham Lincoln made a bold move, declaring nearly four million slaves in ten Confederate states free through his Emancipation Proclamation. Though many think of the Proclamation as the moment of freedom for those who had been enslaved in the United States, the reality is their battle for freedom was far longer and more complicated.

RECONSTRUCTION

After the end of the Civil War in 1865, the United States government had to decide how to enforce the ideals laid out in the Emancipation Proclamation. Congress tackled this problem of forcing states into freeing slaves with the passing of three new constitutional amendments.

The Thirteenth Amendment formally abolished slavery in the United States, declaring all slaves officially free in the eyes of the law, even in the South. The amendment was passed by Congress on January 31, 1865, and ratified by the states on December 6, 1865.

RISE OF THE KU KLUX KLAN

After the end of the Civil War, during Reconstruction, racial tensions were high, especially in the South. Slaves were now free, and the

During the Reconstruction Era, angry whites in the South formed the Ku Klux Klan, a group that terrorized African Americans. The Klan has carried out acts of violence against African Americans and others for decades. Here, an initiation ceremony is shown.

dynamic between freed slaves and their former masters was confusing and, for many on both sides, frightening.

In 1866, a group of white men that included many Confederate veterans founded the Ku Klux Klan in Pulaski, Tennessee. The Klan started as a social club and, fed by the anger and resentment of Southern whites, grew to become a political organization. The group's main goal was to lead the resistance against Reconstruction policies designed to give newly freed slaves equality under the law.

The Klan carried out its mission mostly through violence and intimidation. Dressed in white robes and hoods to mask their identities and often acting at night, they carried out violent acts such as murders, lynchings, arson, and other crimes. They targeted African American homes, schools, and churches, as well as whites who supported African American freedom.

In 1871, the federal government enacted the Ku Klux Klan Act, designed to stop the wave of crime and terror brought on by the Klan. It treated Klan crimes as federal offenses and stifled the group for many years.

The Klan rose and dropped from prominence in the United States over the next century. In 1915, D. W. Griffith's film *Birth of a Nation*, which romanticized the Klan and its actions, sparked a resurgence of the group. The group grew even larger and stronger (and more violent) during the 1960s as the civil rights movement escalated in the South.

Today, many see the Klan as a fringe group of extremists, and its numbers have decreased significantly since the years of the civil rights movement.

In 1868, Congress gave further protection under the law to former slaves by passing the Fourteenth Amendment. The amendment gave citizenship to "all persons born or naturalized in the United States," including former slaves. And it went even further, forbidding states from denying any person

PLESSY V. FERGUSON

Homer Plessy didn't know he was about to make history when he took a seat in the whites-only car of the East Louisiana Railroad in June 1892. The thirty-year-old African American had a light skin complexion due to his Creole heritage (his ancestors were French, Spanish, and Caribbean settlers of Louisiana). With his light skin, he could often pass for white, even though he was considered black under Louisiana law and therefore was required to sit in the "colored" car. When Plessy sat in the white car, he made it clear that he was not white and was promptly arrested for violating the segregation law outlined in the Louisiana Separate Car Act. Plessy's case went all the way to the Supreme Court of the United States. His lawyer argued that the Louisiana act violated the Thirteenth and Fourteenth Amendments. But in 1896, the Supreme Court decided in a 7–1 decision against Plessy, upholding the Louisiana law. The *Plessy v. Ferguson* decision set the precedent for the "separate but equal" doctrine. Separate but equal was the practice that segregated races in separate facilities such as schools, buses, and theaters—as long as the facilities were equal. The unfortunate truth was that facilities for African Americans were rarely equal and were very often inferior, such as African American schools in which students were forced to use outdated textbooks. The effects of *Plessy v. Ferguson* and separate but equal lasted for decades, until 1954 and the *Brown v. Board of Education of Topeka, Kansas*, decision.

"life, liberty or property, without due process of law," or to deny any person equal protection under the laws. By addressing the states, the amendment set a precedent that would be very important decades later during the civil rights era.

The third of this trio of amendments was the Fifteenth, which gave African American men the right to vote. The amendment was ratified on February 3, 1870. However, because of Jim Crow–era tactics, such as poll taxes and literacy tests designed to prevent African Americans from voting in the South, most African Americans in this region were unable to vote until nearly a century later, when the Voting Rights Act of 1965 was passed.

SEPARATE AND UNEQUAL

After the *Plessy v. Ferguson* Supreme Court decision, separate but equal became the status quo in many states. Segregation was enforced in these states through new legislation dubbed Jim Crow laws (named for an African American character in minstrel shows, which were comedy shows of the time that featured white people performing negative stereotypes of African Americans while wearing blackface makeup).

Jim Crow laws were designed to keep African Americans and whites from mingling in public spaces. Separate facilities of all sorts—everything from schools and restaurants to swimming pools and water fountains—were created. Most of these separate facilities were labeled with signs designating which race could use them—either "whites only" or "colored [the antiquated term used to describe African Americans] only."

In other venues or facilities that were harder to separate—such as theaters, buses, and restaurants—sections were created

After the *Plessy v. Ferguson* decision upheld the doctrine of "separate but equal" facilities for whites and African Americans, segregation became the norm across the South. Theaters, water fountains, schools, and other facilities were segregated.

for each race. African Americans were usually forced to sit in the balcony in movie theaters, in the back of buses, or in a separate, partitioned area of restaurants. In some states, African Americans and whites were even forbidden to be buried in the same graveyards, and interracial marriages were illegal in many states as well.

Mentally, emotionally, and socially, this forced segregation left many African Americans feeling as though they were inferior or at least treated as such under the law. They felt this way for good reason. Many of the facilities set aside for

African Americans were older than and inferior to those used by whites. Students in African American–only schools were often forced to use outdated textbooks discarded by the white schools and to sit in classrooms that were overcrowded and in need of repair. And some were forced to travel long distances away from their homes to attend school, even though a whites-only school was near their neighborhood. African Americans who were traveling or in an unfamiliar town were often forced to go without eating or to sleep in their cars because there were no restaurants or hotels that would serve them. Even doing something as simple as seeing a movie was nearly impossible for some African Americans who were unable to climb the stairs to the balcony of the theater, a place that was usually unbearably hot in the summer, and most theaters did not have air conditioning.

In addition to segregation laws, other laws and practices were adopted in many states to discourage or prohibit African Americans from exercising their right to vote. In 1871, Georgia was the first state to enact a poll tax, a tax charged to registered voters. Those who did not pay the tax were not allowed to vote. The tax was only a dollar or two per year, but that was a far more significant amount of money in those days, especially for many African Americans who were poor sharecroppers.

Another tactic used to discourage or prohibit African Americans from voting was the literacy test. The first case of this was South Carolina's eight-box ballot, established in 1882. Voters were forced to put separate ballots for separate offices in individual boxes, and any ballot placed in the wrong box (such as a ballot for senator placed in the governor's box) would be thrown out. The order of the boxes was continuously

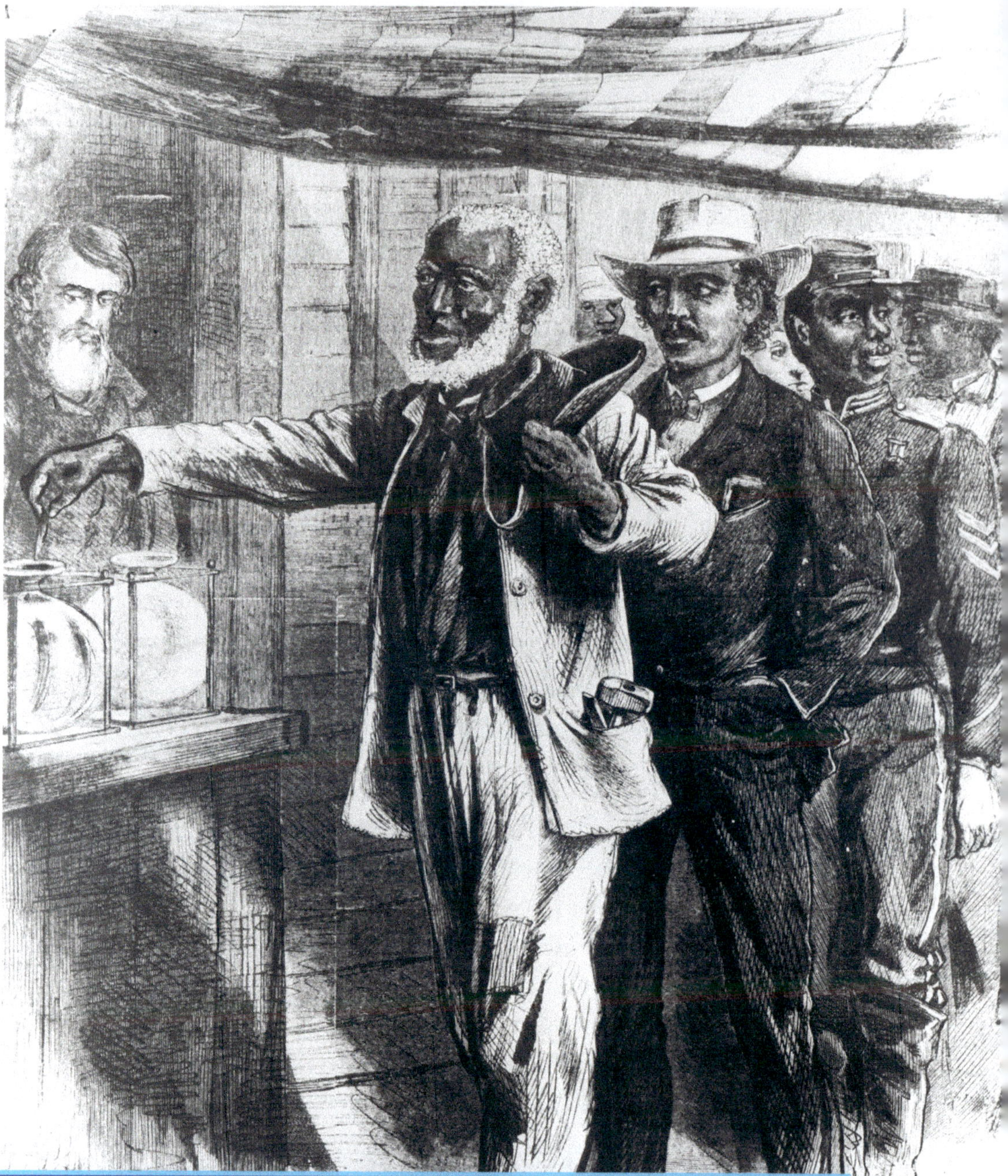

During Reconstruction, many Southern states used tactics such as poll taxes and literacy tests to prevent African American men from exercising their right to vote.

shuffled so that literate voters could not assist illiterate voters in casting their ballot. Once secret ballots were established, states started using literacy tests that were more like a school test to weed out voters who could not read. Poor, illiterate whites protested this move, since it would mean that they also could not vote. So states adopted an "understanding clause" or "grandfather clause," which allowed voters who failed the literacy test to vote as long as they could show the registrar that they understood. Whites could also use this clause if they were descended from someone who was eligible to vote in 1867, the year before African American men were given the right to vote. Since illiterate African Americans far outnumbered illiterate whites, these rules were designed specifically to prevent African Americans from voting.

Though the Emancipation Proclamation and subsequent legislation ensured some freedom for African Americans, many states made it clear that they had a long way to go before they could truly be free.

Chapter 2

FIGHTING FOR FREEDOM

After years of segregation and unequal treatment under Jim Crow laws, many African Americans across the nation, particularly in the South, were ready for things to change. Largely led by young people, a movement of peaceful protests began across the nation. These protests earned a great deal of national attention and in some cases elicited violent reactions. The bravery of these protesters set off a wave of peaceful protests that became the civil rights movement.

PEACEFUL PROTESTS

During the 1950s, the United States was enjoying an era of rebirth and prosperity in the aftermath of World War II. But not all Americans felt that same sense of freedom and prosperity. African Americans, many of whom had fought valiantly in World War II, were growing more and more disenchanted with a country that treated them as second-class citizens. With the inequality created by Jim Crow laws and segregation, African Americans lived a life very different from that of their white counterparts.

In 1955, an African American woman in Montgomery, Alabama, decided to take a stand against inequality and ended up making history. On December 1, 1955, Rosa Parks was riding the city bus home from her job as a seamstress. She sat near the middle of the bus, just behind the first ten seats, which were reserved for whites as part of Jim Crow laws. The seats for whites quickly filled, and when a white man got on the bus, the driver told Parks to give up her seat and move to the back. Parks quietly refused and was arrested for violating segregation laws. In response, local civil rights groups led by a young minister named Martin Luther King Jr. organized a

Rosa Parks *(center, right)* set off the Montgomery Bus Boycott protest when she refused to give up her seat on a Montgomery, Alabama, bus to a white passenger. The boycott helped desegregate the city's bus system.

CIVIL RIGHTS LEADERS

During the civil rights movement, a number of individuals stepped forward to lead protesters and activists in the fight for freedom and equality. Some of these individuals became iconic leaders, making history and leaving a legacy that lives on today.

- **Dr. Martin Luther King Jr.** A Baptist minister from Atlanta, King got involved in the civil rights movement during the 1950s and became the leader of the Southern Christian Leadership Conference. King led numerous peaceful protests, including the Montgomery Bus Boycott and the March on Washington, where he delivered his inspiring "I Have a Dream" speech. In 1964, King was awarded the Nobel Peace Prize at the age of thirty-five, making him the youngest man to ever win the award. King was assassinated on April 4, 1968, in Memphis. King's birthday was eventually declared a national holiday.
- **Medgar Evers** Born and raised in Mississippi, Evers applied to the University of Mississippi Law School, but he was rejected because the school was whites-only. This inspired Evers to get involved with the NAACP's efforts to integrate the university. Evers became a leader in the organization, becoming the NAACP's first field secretary for Mississippi. His activism made him a target for those who opposed civil rights, and in June 1963, he was murdered by segregationist Byron De La Beckwith. The story of Evers's death and the eventual prosecution of Beckwith was told in the 1996 film *Ghosts of Mississippi*.
- **Malcolm X** Born Malcolm Little in Omaha, Nebraska, Malcolm X was a more militant civil rights activist, known for his mantra of obtaining freedom and respect "by any means necessary." The son

A minister from Atlanta, Georgia, Dr. Martin Luther King Jr. was one of the most dynamic leaders of the civil rights movement. His "I Have a Dream" speech inspired crowds at the March on Washington in 1963.

of a civil rights activist, Malcolm X experienced racism and threats throughout his childhood. During his teen and young adult years, he got involved in crime and spent time in jail. During his incarceration, he became involved in the Nation of Islam—a small sect of black Muslims who embraced the ideology of black nationalism (the idea that in order to secure freedom and equality, African Americans needed to establish their own state separate from white Americans). Malcolm X became a leader in the Nation of Islam, but his life was cut short when he was assassinated in 1965. His legacy was carried on through the book *The Autobiography of Malcolm X: As Told to Alex Haley*, published after his death. A film about his life, titled *Malcolm X*, was released in 1992.

bus boycott in Montgomery. Since African Americans made up 75 percent of the bus riders in Montgomery, the boycott presented a serious financial threat to the bus company.

After four students staged a peaceful sit-in protest at a segregated Woolworth lunch counter in Greensboro, North Carolina, sit-in protests were staged by African Americans at lunch counters across the South.

The boycott lasted until December 1956, when the Supreme Court deemed the segregation law unconstitutional and integrated the bus system.

Parks's spirit of quiet protest was picked up in 1960 by four students from North Carolina A&T State University in Greensboro, North Carolina. On February 1 of that year, David Richmond, Franklin McCain, Ezell Blair Jr., and Joseph McNeil walked from their dormitory to the Woolworth in downtown Greensboro. They went upstairs to the department store's whites-only lunch counter, sat down, and ordered coffee. The students were refused service and told to leave, but they refused and stayed in their seats until the store closed.

The next day, the students—dubbed the Greensboro Four—returned with around two dozen of their classmates to continue their protest. They sat for hours, quietly studying as they were heckled by white customers. The protest caught the attention of the media, and pretty soon, hundreds of young African Americans filled the Greensboro Woolworth, as well as Woolworth stores and other segregated lunch counters across the country. The sit-in movement was born.

In July 1960, the Greensboro Woolworth's lunch counter was officially desegregated. Lunch counters across the nation followed suit.

In 1961, civil rights activists dubbed Freedom Riders rode buses throughout the South, visiting restaurants, bus stations, and other facilities to test whether they were upholding the 1960 Supreme Court decision that deemed segregated facilities for interstate passengers illegal.

The next year, hundreds of volunteers—mostly young people, both African American and white—began testing a 1960 Supreme Court decision that deemed segregated

CIVIL RIGHTS ORGANIZATIONS

As the civil rights movement took off, several organizations dedicated to fighting for equality for African Americans became more important than ever. One of the largest and best known of these groups is the National Association for the Advancement of Colored People (NAACP). Founded in 1909, the NAACP's mission is to ensure the political, educational, social, and economic equality of rights of all persons and to eliminate race-based discrimination. The NAACP supported many of the movement's largest protests, including the Montgomery Bus Boycott and the March on Washington. The NAACP continues to work for equality today.

Another important group during the civil rights movement was the Congress of Racial Equality (CORE). Founded in 1942, the group believed in peaceful protests as exemplified by Indian leader Mohandas (Mahatma) Gandhi. CORE was instrumental in organizing Freedom Rides and the March on Washington.

The Southern Christian Leadership Conference (SCLC) was founded in Atlanta and led for several years by Dr. Martin Luther King Jr. The SCLC worked within churches across the South to organize and support peaceful civil rights protests.

More militant was the Black Panther Party, an organization founded in 1966 under the principles of black nationalism. The group was initially formed to help protect African American neighborhoods and African Americans from police brutality. The Panthers instituted programs to help the African American community, but they also received a great deal of criticism for their militant stance and ties to socialist ideals.

These organizations, and others like them, allowed civil rights activists and regular citizens to get involved and organize their efforts in the fight for equality.

facilities for interstate passengers illegal. They boarded buses and traveled throughout the South for seven months in 1961, visiting whites-only waiting rooms and restaurants in bus stations. These protesters were called Freedom Riders.

During their rides, the Freedom Riders faced violence and intimidation from mobs of angry locals in Southern states. In May 1961, an angry mob surrounded a bus in Alabama, throwing bricks and rocks and even throwing a firebomb through one of the bus windows. Similar acts of violence occurred in other Southern cities.

In August 1963, one of the largest and most memorable protests occurred in Washington, D.C. The March on Washington for Jobs and Freedom brought more than 200,000 people of all races to the Washington Mall in an effort to highlight the challenges faced by African Americans.

Organized by various civil and religious groups, the march culminated with the now famous "I Have a Dream" speech by Dr. Martin Luther King Jr. A Baptist minister from the South, King solidified his status as one of the leaders of the peaceful protest movement by electrifying the crowd with his words of freedom and equality for all, delivered on the steps of the Lincoln Memorial.

VIOLENT RESPONSE

Though most of the protests during the civil rights movement were peaceful, many of them were met with violence. In addition to the angry mobs that attacked Freedom Riders in the South, other violent reactions were directed to many of those working to bring equality and freedom to all Americans.

Civil rights activist Medgar Evers was one of the first activists to be assassinated when he was shot in the driveway of his home in Jackson, Mississippi, by a segregationist in 1963.

In 1963, tensions hit an all-time high between civil rights protesters and those who did not want African Americans to receive equal treatment under the law. Violence erupted all across the South, in particular, with the Ku Klux Klan and other groups using violence to intimidate those working for civil rights.

During that year, two major events occurred that shed a new light onto the violence and hatred that was running rampant in the South.

In June 1963, civil rights activist Medgar Evers was returning to his Jackson, Mississippi, home one evening when he was shot and killed in his own driveway. Evers, who was a prominent member of the NAACP, had become a target for his work organizing voter drives and other protests in Mississippi. Evers and his family had been threatened numerous times.

The Federal Bureau of Investigation (FBI) looked into the murder and quickly determined a suspect—Byron Beckwith, a white segregationist and founding member of Mississippi's White Citizens Council. Even though a great deal of evidence pointed to Beckwith as the killer, he was set free in 1964 after two all-white juries deadlocked. Beckwith was finally convicted of the crime in 1994, thirty-one years after Evers's death.

A few months later in 1963, another horrific crime shocked the nation. Just after 10 AM on September 15, 1963, the Ku Klux Klan bombed the 16th Street Baptist Church in Birmingham, Alabama. Four young girls—Addie Mae Collins (age fourteen), Denise McNair (age eleven), Carole Robertson (age fourteen), and Cynthia Wesley (age fourteen)—were killed in the explosion, and twenty-two others were injured.

Witnesses named Klansman Robert Chambliss as the man who planted the bomb at the church. He was arrested but was only charged for having dynamite without a permit and just had to pay a fine and serve a six-month jail sentence. Chambliss was finally tried and convicted of the bombing and murders in 1977. He was found guilty and received a life sentence, of which he served less than ten years as he was seventy-three years old at sentencing.

These horrific acts of violence stunned many people across the nation. President John F. Kennedy expressed his shock and concern over what was going on in the South, and people of all races spoke out against the violence against innocent people. The shocking nature of these crimes, and other violent acts of the era, began to change minds and set the stage for major changes in the United States.

Chapter 3

EARLY LEGISLATION

Years before the Civil Rights Act of 1964, several other pieces of legislation helped lay the groundwork for this monumental act. These early legislative decisions started the hard-fought fight for equality and freedom for African Americans.

FEDERAL INTERVENTION

As tensions began to rise in the South, the federal government decided it was time to address the issue of inequality. One of the first moves occurred in 1957, when President Dwight D. Eisenhower sent the U.S. Congress a proposal for civil rights legislation. That proposal led to the passing of the Civil Rights Act of 1957.

The Civil Rights Act of 1957 accomplished several goals, including the establishment of a civil rights division of the Justice Department to uphold the civil and constitutional rights of all Americans. The Justice Department's civil rights division also enforces federal statutes prohibiting discrimination on the basis of race, color, sex, disability, religion, familial

President Dwight D. Eisenhower passed early civil rights legislation with the Civil Rights Act of 1957. While a good step forward, the act was not comprehensive enough to solve all the country's civil rights problems.

status, and national origin. The division was instrumental in the investigations of murdered civil rights leaders such as Medgar Evers.

Also established as part of the Civil Rights Act of 1957 was the U.S. Commission on Civil Rights. The commission

THE CIVIL RIGHTS DIVISION OF THE DEPARTMENT OF JUSTICE

Although it wasn't particularly aggressive in its pursuit of civil rights violations in its early years, the Civil Rights Division of the Department of Justice has become an important ally for those fighting for equal rights in the United States. The division, which was created in 1957 by the enactment of the Civil Rights Act of 1957, works to uphold the civil and constitutional rights of all Americans. The division enforces federal statutes prohibiting discrimination on the basis of race, color, sex, disability, religion, familial status, and national origin.

Since its infancy, the division has grown dramatically in both size and scope and has played a major role in many of the nation's most important civil rights battles. Lawyers from the division prosecuted the defendants accused of murdering three civil rights workers in Mississippi in 1964 and were involved in the investigations of the assassinations of civil rights leaders Dr. Martin Luther King Jr. and Medgar Evers. The Civil Rights Division enforces a wide variety of laws that protect the civil rights of all Americans.

Today, the Civil Rights Division is led by acting assistant attorney general Jocelyn Samuels. Based in Washington, D.C., the division is broken into sections led by section chiefs, deputy chiefs, and special legal or litigation counsels.

is an independent, bipartisan, fact-finding federal agency that works to inform the development of national civil rights policy and enhance enforcement of federal civil rights laws. The commission's work includes studying alleged deprivations of voting rights and alleged discrimination based on race, color, religion, sex, age, disability, or national origin, or in the administration of justice. The commission also plays a vital role in advancing civil rights through objective and comprehensive investigation, research, and analysis on issues of fundamental concern to the federal government and the public.

While it was an important step forward in the struggle for equality, the Civil Rights Act of 1957 wasn't especially effective. The act was weakened by a lack of support in Congress, and while it did establish agencies meant to address the problems of racism and discrimination, it did not directly prohibit the discrimination that was rampant in the South.

LEGAL BATTLES

The fight for equality was waged in another important arena during the civil rights movement—the courtroom. Several monumental cases brought major changes to laws in the United States.

One of the first cases to address the issue of inequality was *Brown v. Board of Education of Topeka, Kansas,* in 1954. Though the case was named for Oliver Brown—an African American father who sued the school board in his town so that his daughter could attend an all-white school in their neighborhood—the Supreme Court case actually encompassed five cases from around the nation that challenged the

Elizabeth Eckford, one of the nine African American students who tried to integrate Little Rock Central High School in Little Rock, Arkansas, faced angry crowds of whites who were opposed to desegregating the school.

constitutionality of segregated schools. The Court ultimately ruled that the "separate but equal" doctrine was unconstitutional and that schools should be desegregated.

But the desegregation of schools, especially in the South, was a slow process. In 1957, the ruling was tested in Little Rock, Arkansas, when nine African American students—dubbed the Little Rock Nine—enrolled at the city's Central High School. On the day they were to start school, the students were blocked by the Arkansas National Guard, called in by Arkansas governor Orval Faubus. In the following weeks, the NAACP filed an injunction that was granted and the Arkansas National Guard was told to let the students enter the

JUSTICE EARL WARREN

Serving as the chief justice of the U.S. Supreme Court, Justice Earl Warren made history in 1954 presiding over the landmark *Brown v. Board of Education* decision. The historic moment was many years in the making for the influential justice.

A native of California, Warren spent many years as a lawyer, including fourteen years as the Alameda County district attorney. He

U.S. Supreme Court Chief Justice Earl Warren made history in 1954 when he presided over the *Brown v. Board of Education* decision that ruled school segregation illegal.

was then elected governor of California for three consecutive terms from 1942 to 1953. Warren was also the vice presidential candidate in 1948 alongside presidential candidate Thomas Dewey.

In 1953, President Dwight Eisenhower appointed Warren to the Supreme Court as the chief justice. In addition to his work on the court, Warren led the commission that investigated the assassination of President John F. Kennedy.

Warren retired in 1969 and died on July 9, 1974, in Washington, D.C.

school. Angry mobs greeted the students with taunts and threats of violence, and they were escorted in with police protection and, eventually, federal troops and National Guardsmen sent by President Eisenhower to help control the mobs.

In 1956, the Supreme Court also upheld a lower court ruling in the case of Rosa Parks and the Montgomery Bus Boycott. The lower court ruled that segregation in the Montgomery bus system was illegal, and without comment the Supreme Court upheld that decision, giving a huge victory to Parks and Dr. Martin Luther King Jr., who were the leaders of the boycott.

Chapter 4

A HISTORIC ACT

When he came into office in 1961, President John F. Kennedy was initially slow to support new antidiscrimination measures. But with tensions coming to a violent head in the South, President Kennedy realized it was time to do something to address the issues being raised by the civil rights movement.

KENNEDY'S MOVE

In the wake of horrific violence, such as the bombing of the 16th Street Baptist Church in Birmingham, the murder of civil rights activist Medgar Evers, and police brutality against nonviolent protesters, President Kennedy realized things were terribly out of hand in the South. Though he'd been largely hands-off regarding the civil rights movement during his first few years in office, he realized the time had come to do something.

In June 1963, Alabama governor George Wallace upheld his promise to "stand in the schoolhouse door" to prevent two black students from enrolling at the University of Alabama.

Alabama governor George Wallace was a segregationist and attempted to block integration at the University of Alabama in 1963.

To protect the students and permit their admission, President Kennedy federalized the Alabama National Guard. And on June 11, the president addressed the nation, calling the fight over civil rights a moral, constitutional, and legal fight. He then proposed civil rights legislation that was far more comprehensive than anything previously considered. Saying the United States "will not be fully free until all of its citizens are free," Kennedy's legislation was written to guarantee equal access to public facilities, to end segregation in schools, and to provide federal protection of the right to vote.

KENNEDY: UNLIKELY ACTIVIST

While he came from a privileged New England background in one of the nation's most famous families, President John F. Kennedy felt a strong kinship with the African Americans fighting for equality during the civil rights movement.

During his 1960 presidential campaign, Kennedy and his brother Senator Robert F. Kennedy came to the assistance of Dr. Martin Luther King Jr., who had been unjustly arrested while leading a protest in Atlanta. President Kennedy called King's wife, Coretta, and asked Robert to call in a favor to the judge to get King released. The showing of support helped earn Kennedy more than 70 percent of the African American vote in the election, helping him become president.

However, once in office, Kennedy was cautious because of the narrow margin of his victory and a lack of support in Congress. While he genuinely cared about civil rights and voiced his support for desegregating schools, he was resistant to taking strong action on civil rights for fear of the controversy it would start.

The summer of 1963 changed that. Violence in the South was out of control, with even the police and government officials participating in violence and working to discriminate against African Americans. President Kennedy was disturbed by what he saw happening and knew the time to act was upon him. After telling the Alabama National Guard to come to the assistance of African American students trying to desegregate the University of Alabama, Kennedy debuted his proposed civil rights legislation to the nation and Congress.

The legislation would go on to change the course of history in the United States and bring equality to African Americans across the nation. But Kennedy would not live to see his legislation become law.

President John F. Kennedy *(third from right)* was an important ally of civil rights activists such as Dr. Martin Luther King Jr. *(far left).* Kennedy proposed the legislation that became the Civil Rights Act of 1964.

On November 22, 1963, Kennedy was shot by Lee Harvey Oswald during a parade in Dallas, Texas. Though he did not live to see his legislation through to the end, his brave move to bring equal rights to all made him one of the most important figures of the civil rights movement.

The proposed legislation became the subject of hearings by the House Judiciary Committee and was amended during the hearings to broaden its scope of protections. The House Judiciary Committee approved the legislation on October 26, 1963, and formally reported it to the full House on November 20, 1963. Two days later, President Kennedy was assassinated in Dallas, Texas.

SURVIVING AN ASSASSINATION

In the wake of President John F. Kennedy's assassination in 1963, the world seemed to be in chaos. And amid that chaos, some worried that Kennedy's civil rights legislation would be lost without the president to champion it through Congress.

But former vice president and newly sworn-in president Lyndon B. Johnson immediately made a commitment to carry out Kennedy's legislative agenda, including the civil rights legislation. In his first State of the Union address as president, Johnson said, "Let this session of Congress be known as the session which did more for civil rights than the last hundred sessions combined."

With the president's support, the bill was introduced to the U.S. House of Representatives. The bill was immediately met with opposition from Southern representatives. Debates were held in the House, and Southern representatives argued that the bill was unconstitutional because it infringed on personal liberty and states' rights.

In an attempt to kill the bill, Southern segregationists introduced "hostile amendments"—amendments designed to change or defeat the purpose of a bill. More than one hundred hostile amendments were introduced and defeated by

West Virginia senator Robert C. Byrd, a former Ku Klux Klan member, spoke for more than fourteen hours in an attempt to filibuster the Civil Rights Act of 1964 and prevent it from passing.

the House. Eventually, the House passed the bill with support from both Republicans and Democrats by a vote of 290–130.

Once the bill passed in the House, it was sent to the Senate. In the Senate, the bill faced its greatest opposition yet. Southern and border-state Democrats staged a fifty-four-day filibuster (a debate that is extended for an extremely long period in an attempt to kill legislation, usually by one person talking continuously on the Senate floor), which was one of the longest in history. At one point during the filibuster, Senator Robert Byrd of West Virginia—who was a former Ku Klux Klan member—spoke for more than fourteen consecutive hours.

But behind the scenes, supporters of the bill negotiated and cut deals with fellow members of the Senate to earn their votes. With enough support to finally end the filibuster, the Senate voted to pass the bill by a vote of 73–27 in favor. One senator—Senator Clair Engle of California—was too sick to speak from suffering with a brain tumor, but he signaled his yes vote by pointing to his eye.

THE BILL BECOMES LAW

President Johnson signed the bill into law on July 2, 1964. Just as President Kennedy had hoped, the Civil Rights Act of 1964 was the most comprehensive civil rights legislation ever passed in the United States. Its provisions ensured equal rights for all Americans and changed many laws, especially in the South. The law included these provisions:

Title I—Voting Rights: This provision barred unequal voter registration requirements but did not abolish the use of literacy tests sometimes used to prevent African Americans and poor whites from voting.

Title II—Public Accommodations: This provision outlawed discrimination in public venues engaging in interstate commerce, such as hotels, motels, restaurants, and theaters.

Title III—Desegregation of Public Facilities: This provision made it possible for lawsuits brought by the Justice Department to secure desegregation of certain public facilities.

Title IV—Desegregation of Public Education: This provision desegregated public schools, both K–12 and colleges, and authorized the U.S. Attorney General to file lawsuits to force desegregation in cases where schools did not do so automatically.

Title V—Civil Rights Commission: This provision addressed the procedures for the commission and broadened its duties.

Title VI—Nondiscrimination in Federally Assisted Programs: This provision authorized withdrawal of federal funds from programs that practiced discrimination.

Title VII—Equal Employment Opportunity: This provision prohibits discrimination in employment on the bases of race, color, national origin, religion, and sex. Title VII also created the Equal Employment Opportunity Commission to implement the law.

Title VIII—Registration and Voting Statistics: This provision directed the Census Bureau to collect registration and voting statistics based on race but specified that individuals did not have to share that information with the Bureau.

Title IX—Intervention and Removal of Cases: This provision made it possible for federal high courts to review the

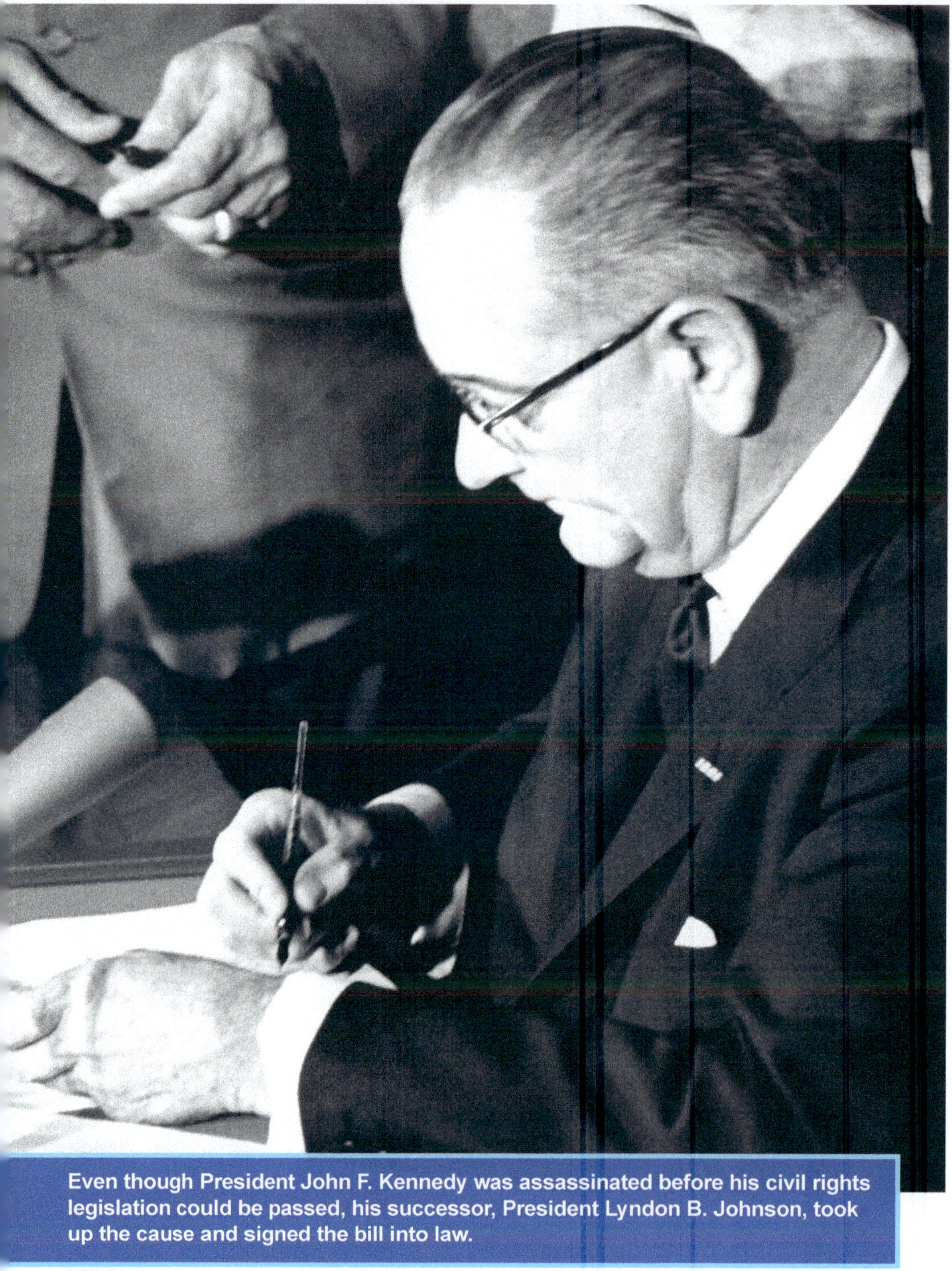

Even though President John F. Kennedy was assassinated before his civil rights legislation could be passed, his successor, President Lyndon B. Johnson, took up the cause and signed the bill into law.

decisions of federal district courts in civil rights cases and authorized the attorney general to intervene when necessary in private lawsuits.

Title X—Community Relations Service: This provision created the Community Relations Service, which helped communities resolve disputes relating to racial discrimination.

The provisions of the law meant major changes in the lives of Americans, especially African Americans living in the segregated South. No longer were there whites-only facilities that African Americans were not permitted to use. African Americans could no longer be denied service in restaurants or lunch counters based upon the color of their skin. And schools were no longer to be segregated—white and African American children would learn together in schools across the nation.

While the Civil Rights Act of 1964 was a monumental piece of legislation that drastically changed the lives of millions of Americans for the better, it wasn't the final word in ending discrimination in the United States. It would take years for some of the provisions of the act to be enforced, and additional legislation would be needed to bring full equality to all.

Chapter 5

AN ENDURING LEGACY

The passing of the Civil Rights Act of 1964 set the stage for continuing changes in the United States. In the years after the bill's passage, additional legislation was passed to stop discrimination against several other groups and to ensure equality in all areas of life for every American.

OPENING THE DOOR TO EQUALITY

The Civil Rights Act of 1964 was the first in a series of legislation that brought equality to Americans who had previously been subject to discrimination. In the year following the passage of the bill, a new piece of legislation was introduced that expanded and protected freedoms further.

Mere weeks before the signing of the Civil Rights Act of 1964, three civil rights activists working to register African Americans to vote in Mississippi were murdered by members of the Ku Klux Klan. Months later, in March 1965, voting rights activists staged a peaceful march from Selma, Alabama, to

The Selma to Montgomery March, led by Dr. Martin Luther King Jr., was a peaceful protest for voting rights that went wrong when local law enforcement brutally attacked the protestors.

the state capital in Montgomery. During the march, Alabama State Troopers descended on the group, attacking them with nightsticks, tear gas, and whips when they refused to leave. Some of the protesters were severely beaten, and the attack was caught on camera and broadcast on the news.

In response to the brutal attack, President Johnson called for voting rights legislation. Addressing Congress, he spoke of the various ways that election officials in the South prohibited African Americans from voting—literacy tests and even outright lies, such as telling voters they'd gotten the day wrong and missed their chance to vote. Some African Americans were even asked to recite the Constitution or explain complicated provisions of state laws in order to vote—all but guaranteeing they would not be able to complete the difficult task—and were thus denied the right to vote. It was clear that additional legislation was necessary to ensure that African Americans in the South would be able to exercise their right to vote.

President Johnson's proposed voting rights legislation was made into a bill that was introduced to the U.S. Senate in spring 1965. With little opposition, the bill was passed in the Senate by a 77–19 vote on May 26, 1965. The legislation was met with a bit more opposition in the House of Representatives. But after debating the bill for more than a month, the House passed the legislation by a vote of 333–85 on July 9, 1965. President Johnson signed the Voting Rights Act into law on August 6, with Martin Luther King Jr. and other civil rights leaders standing by at the ceremony.

The Voting Rights Act of 1965 resolved all of the issues that were left open after the Civil Rights Act of 1964. The new law banned the use of literacy tests, provided for federal oversight of voter registration in areas where less than 50 percent of the nonwhite population had not registered to vote, and authorized the U.S. Attorney General to investigate the use of poll taxes in state and local elections. In 1964, the Twenty-Fourth Amendment made poll taxes illegal in federal elections, yet there were still reports of the taxes being used, especially in state elections. In 1966, the U.S. Supreme Court banned poll taxes in state elections.

Even though the Voting Rights Act of 1965 was signed into law, it did not necessarily mean instant changes, especially in the South. At the state and local levels, particularly in the South, enforcement of the law was weak, and it was often ignored. In areas where the number of African Americans in the population was high and their vote threatened the political power of whites, the law faced resistance. But even in those situations, the Voting Rights Act gave African American voters the legal standing to challenge voting restrictions and greatly improved voter turnout among African Americans. In the state of Mississippi alone, voter turnout among African Americans increased significantly—from 6 percent in 1964 to 59 percent in 1969.

Since its passage nearly fifty years ago, the Voting Rights Act has been amended to offer additional protections, such as the guarantee of voting rights for non-English-speaking American citizens.

With the passage of the Civil Rights Act of 1964 and the Voting Rights Act of 1965, African Americans and other minorities were experiencing more freedom and equality than ever before. But there was still work to be done.

For decades, neighborhoods in many areas were segregated —whites lived around other whites, and African Americans and other minorities were not welcome to move into all-white

The Fair Housing Act expanded the Civil Rights Act of 1964 and addressed the issue of fair housing practices for African Americans, making it illegal for anyone to be denied housing based on race.

neighborhoods or apartment buildings. Several Supreme Court decisions, including *Shelley v. Kraemer* in 1948 and *Jones v. Mayer Co.* in June 1968, prohibited the exclusion of African Americans or other minorities from certain sections of cities. But even with those decisions, race-based housing patterns were still very common even in the late 1960s, and those who challenged these segregated neighborhoods were often met with resistance and, in some cases, violence.

Also during the late 1960s, the Vietnam War was raging. A significant number of African American and other minority soldiers fought and died in Vietnam. But despite that sacrifice, many of these soldiers' families experienced difficulty renting or buying homes in certain neighborhoods because of their race. Because of this, organizations such as the NAACP, the G.I. Forum, and the National Committee Against Discrimination in Housing started working to get new fair housing legislation passed.

Legislation was proposed in 1968 to expand upon the Civil Rights Act of 1964. Originally, the bill was designed to extend federal protection to civil rights workers, but it was also expanded to address racial discrimination in housing. Title VIII of the proposed legislation was known as the Fair Housing Act, and that was eventually used as a shorthand description for the entire bill. The bill prohibited discrimination regarding the sale, rental, and financing of housing based on race, religion, national origin, and sex.

Once the bill was sent to the Senate, it became subject to debate. During the arguments, Senator Edward Brooke of Massachusetts—the first African American ever elected to the Senate by popular vote—shared the story of his return from serving in World War II and not being able to find the home

Massachusetts Senator Edward Brooke, the first African American elected to the Senate by popular vote, shared his story of being unable to find housing after returning from World War II during the deliberation of the Fair Housing Act.

he wanted for his family because of his race. Despite this emotional argument, the bill still faced a filibuster by Southern senators. But with the support of Senate Republican leader Everett Dirksen, the bill was passed in a close vote.

The bill then moved on to the House of Representatives, where it was expected to meet resistance and possibly be weakened because of the conservative leanings of the current representatives. But Congress received unexpected pressure from President Johnson after the assassination of Dr. Martin Luther King Jr. set off a wave of riots and unrest. King had long been an advocate for fair housing rights, and Johnson believed the bill would be a good way to honor King and his legacy and wanted the bill passed before King's funeral. After a shortened debate, the House passed the Fair Housing Act on April 10, 1968, and President Johnson signed it into law the following day.

In 1988, Congress expanded the law, passing the Fair Housing Amendments Act, which prohibited discrimination in housing based on disability or family status (pregnancy or the presence of children under the age of eighteen). These amendments gave control of the enforcement of the Fair Housing Act to the U.S. Department of Housing and Urban Development (HUD), which processes and sends complaints related to housing discrimination to be investigated by the department's Office of Fair Housing and Equal Opportunity (FHEO).

MODERN IMPLICATIONS AND INTERPRETATIONS

In the five decades since the passage of the Civil Rights Act of 1964, the United States has become a very different nation than the one of the 1960s. The law changed the cultural landscape of this country, making it possible for whites and African Americans to intermingle as they had not in the past. People of all races attend the same schools, drink from the same water fountains, use the same restrooms, and eat at the same restaurants, among other things. These changes have broken down many of the social walls that separated the races, allowing people to forge friendships, romantic relationships, and

TITLE IX: DELIVERING EDUCATION EQUALITY

Though it is most commonly known for its role in women's college athletics, Title IX is a far more complex law that protects individuals in a variety of ways in educational settings.

In 1972, a set of amendments known as the Education Amendments of 1972 were signed into law by President Richard Nixon. Title IX of these amendments became one of the most important and impactful pieces of legislation since the Civil Rights Act of 1964.

Title IX is a comprehensive federal law that protects people from discrimination on the basis of sex in any federally funded educational program or activity. It states: "No person in the United States shall, on the basis of sex, be excluded from participation in, be denied the benefits of, or be subjected to discrimination under any education program or activity receiving Federal financial assistance."

The main purpose of Title IX is to prohibit the use of federal money to support sexually discriminatory practices—such as sexual harassment and employment discrimination—in educational programs, as well as to provide individual citizens effective protection against those practices. Title IX applies to state and local agencies that receive funds from the U.S. Department of Education. These agencies include approximately 16,000 local school districts, 3,200 colleges and universities, and 5,000 for-profit schools, in addition to libraries and museums. Other facilities, such as vocational rehabilitation agencies and education agencies, also are included.

The Office for Civil Rights (OCR), which is a part of the Department of Education, is responsible for enforcing Title IX. The OCR makes

Title IX of the Education Amendments of 1972 ensures equality for all students, regardless of race, sex, or any other factor. The legislation is best known for maintaining equality in college athletics.

certain that institutions that receive funds from the Department of Education comply with Title IX through compliance enforcement. The OCR carries out this enforcement primarily through investigation and resolution of complaints filed by people alleging sex discrimination. In addition, the OCR uses agency-initiated reviews of selected recipients to identify and eliminate sex discrimination that may not be addressed through complaint investigations.

In 2012, Title IX celebrated its fortieth anniversary, a major milestone for all those who have received an education free from discrimination and harassment because of its enforcement.

The enduring legacy of the work of civil rights activists was certainly felt in 2008, when President Barack Obama was elected as the nation's first African American president. President Obama is seen here after his re-election, in 2012.

business partnerships that once would have been nearly impossible. Even more amazing in comparison to the cultural climate of the 1960s is the fact that an African American, Barack Obama, was elected as president of the United States in 2008 and re-elected in 2012.

In the years since the passing of the Civil Rights Act of 1964 and subsequent civil rights legislation that occurred in the decade following the act, there have been additional legislation and court decisions that have broadened and modified civil rights laws in the United States.

On March 22, 1988, Congress passed the Civil Rights Restoration Act, broadening the scope of earlier civil rights legislation and clarifying its application.

The act was passed in response to the 1984 Supreme Court ruling in the case of *Grove City College v. Bell*, which determined that Title IX regulations would apply only to the private college's financial aid department, the only department that received federal funding. The Civil Rights Restoration Act overturned this ruling, stating that recipients of federal funds must comply with Title IX regulations in all areas, not just in the certain program or activity that received funds from the federal government.

In more recent times, the fight for civil rights has expanded to include additional groups, particularly gay Americans. Gay rights activists have been campaigning for many years to change laws that prohibit gay Americans from legally marrying and receiving the same benefits and treatment as heterosexual married couples. Since the early 2000s, several states, including Iowa, New York, and Delaware, have legalized gay marriage through court decisions, bills passed in the state legislature, or popular vote.

However, gay marriage has not been legalized by the federal government. Gay rights activists did score a major victory on that front in 2013, when the U.S. Supreme Court struck down a key part of the 1996 Defense of Marriage Act (DOMA). The Court declared that gay couples married in states where gay marriage is legal must receive the same federal health, tax, Social Security, and other benefits received by heterosexual couples. Conservative justice Anthony M. Kennedy joined the Court's four liberal judges in declaring DOMA's prohibition on federal recognition of legally married couples unconstitutional, saying, "DOMA writes inequality into the entire United States Code."

In addition, the Court turned away a case involving California's banning of same-sex marriage, known as Proposition 8, essentially upholding a lower court's decision

The fight for civil rights continues today, particularly with the fight for equality for gay Americans. A major victory in that struggle was won in 2013, when the U.S. Supreme Court deemed the Defense of Marriage Act unconstitutional.

that the ban is unconstitutional. The ruling meant that same-sex marriage would officially be legal in sixteen states and the District of Columbia by the end of that year. For gay rights activists who'd long fought for equal rights, just as civil rights activists did in the 1960s, the rulings brought a sense of victory very much like that felt after the passing of the Civil Rights Act of 1964.

During that same Supreme Court session, another civil rights act was ruled upon, but with very different results. The Court struck down a key component of the Voting Rights Act of 1965 by a 5–4 vote, declaring that nine states (most of which are in the South) could change their election laws without advance federal approval. This rule was set in the original legislation to help prevent these states from using unfair and illegal tactics to prevent African Americans from voting.

In writing for the majority, Chief Justice John G. Roberts said, "Our country has changed. While any racial discrimination in voting is too much, Congress must ensure that the legislation it passes to remedy that problem speaks to current conditions."

Immediately following the decision, several Southern states—such as Texas and North Carolina—enacted new voter ID laws that require voters to present a photo ID before they are allowed to cast their ballot. There has been a great deal of opposition to these laws, since some believe they unfairly target minorities and poor people who are unable to afford or find transportation to obtain a photo ID. The Department of Justice has brought lawsuits against both states over their new voter ID laws.

While it has been more than five decades since civil rights activists such as Martin Luther King Jr., Medgar Evers, Rosa Parks, and the Greensboro Four took a stand against injustice and inequality, the lasting effects of their brave actions live on today. With the passing of the Civil Rights Act of 1964, as well as subsequent civil rights legislation, the efforts of those who struggled and even died fighting for the cause of equal rights were finally validated and rewarded. And their bravery has inspired scores of other activists who've followed in their footsteps, carrying on the fight for equal rights for all.

TIMELINE

1863 Abraham Lincoln's Emancipation Proclamation declares nearly four million slaves free.

1865 The Thirteenth Amendment formally abolishes slavery in the United States.

1866 The Ku Klux Klan forms in Tennessee.

1868 The Fourteenth Amendment gives citizenship to all people born or naturalized in the United States, even slaves.

1870 The Fifteenth Amendment gives African American men the right to vote.

1871 Georgia is the first state to enact a poll tax, designed to prevent African Americans and poor people from voting. The federal government enacts the Ku Klux Klan Act, designed to stop violence perpetrated by the group.

1896 The Supreme Court decision in *Plessy v. Ferguson* establishes the doctrine of "separate but equal."

1909 The NAACP is founded.

1954 The Supreme Court deems segregation in schools illegal in the *Brown v. Board of Education* decision.

1955 Rosa Parks refuses to give up her seat on a bus in Montgomery, Alabama, setting off the Montgomery Bus Boycott.

1957 The Civil Rights Act of 1957 is passed.

1960 Four college students stage the first lunch counter sit-in at the Woolworth in Greensboro, North Carolina. The Supreme Court declares segregated facilities for interstate passengers illegal.

1961 The Freedom Riders test the Supreme Court decision by riding buses through the South and using whites-only facilities in protest of segregation.

1963 Medgar Evers is assassinated. The March on Washington for Jobs and Freedom brings more than two hundred thousand people of all races to the Washington Mall in an effort to highlight the challenges faced by African Americans. The Ku Klux Klan bombs the 16th Street Baptist Church in Birmingham, Alabama, killing four young girls.

President John F. Kennedy proposes comprehensive civil rights legislation. President John F. Kennedy is assassinated in Dallas, Texas.

1964 President Lyndon B. Johnson signs the Civil Rights Act of 1964 into law.

1965 Protesters are attacked by police marching from Selma, Alabama, to Montgomery. The Voting Rights Act of 1965 is passed.

1968 The Fair Housing Act is passed.

GLOSSARY

ABOLITION The act of doing away with something, such as slavery.

AMENDMENT A change in the words or meaning of a law or document.

ASSASSINATION The murder of a high-profile person, usually for political reasons.

BILL A draft of a proposed law.

BLACK NATIONALISM The advocacy of separate national status for African Americans.

BOYCOTT To refuse to buy or use a product or service out of protest.

DISCRIMINATION The unjust treatment of different categories of people on the grounds of race, age, sex, or another trait.

FILIBUSTER A debate that is extended for an extremely long period in an attempt to kill legislation, usually by one person talking continuously on the Senate floor.

INJUNCTION A court order by which an individual is required to perform, or is restrained from performing, a particular act.

INTEGRATION The bringing of people of different racial or ethnic groups into unrestricted and equal association, ending segregation.

JIM CROW LAWS A set of laws in the South designed to segregate African Americans from whites.

LEGISLATION Laws or a collection of laws considered by a legislative body, such as Congress.

LYNCHING The killing of someone illegally, often by hanging at the hands of a mob, as punishment for a crime or perceived crime.

MINORITIES Smaller subsets of the total population; for example, African Americans or Hispanics in the United States.

POLL TAX A tax levied on people rather than on property, often as a requirement for voting.

PROVISION A condition or agreement of a law.

RECONSTRUCTION The reorganization and reestablishment of the seceded states in the Union after the American Civil War.

SEGREGATION The enforced or voluntary separation of groups in public facilities or residential areas on the basis of race, class, or another factor.

SEGREGATIONIST A person who advocated for racial segregation.

SHARECROPPER A tenant farmer who gives a part of each crop as rent.

Birmingham Civil Rights Institute (BCRI)
520 16th Street North
Birmingham, AL 35203
(205) 328-9696, ext. 203
http://bcri.org

The Birmingham Civil Rights Institute documents the struggles of the African American citizens and business and community leaders of Birmingham before, during, and after the civil rights movement. It hosts exhibits and offers educational programs to the public.

British Columbia Civil Liberties Association (BCCLA)
900 Helmcken Street, 2nd floor
Vancouver, BC V6Z 1B3
Canada
(604) 687-2919
Web site: http://bccla.org

The BCCLA defends civil and human rights throughout Canada and promotes public knowledge of its efforts through publications as well as its education, advocacy, public policy, and justice programs.

Canadian Civil Liberties Association (CCLA)
215 Spadina Avenue, Suite 210
Toronto, ON M5T 2C7
Canada
(416) 363-0321
Web site: http://ccla.org

The Canadian Civil Liberties Association defends and promotes awareness of fundamental human rights and civil liberties through public education, research, litigation, and other endeavors.

International Civil Rights Center and Museum
134 S. Elm Street
Greensboro, NC 27401
(336) 274-9199
Web site: http://sitinmovement.org
Housed in the former Woolworth where the first sit-in was staged, this museum celebrates the history and legacy of the civil rights movement, especially the legacy of the brave individuals who participated in the sit-in movement in 1960.

The King Center
449 Auburn Avenue NE
Atlanta, GA 30312
(404) 526-8900
Web site: http://www.thekingcenter.org
The King Center is a memorial museum to the legacy of Dr. Martin Luther King Jr. and a nonprofit group dedicated to providing educational and community programs that embody Dr. King's philosophy and vision.

Leadership Conference on Civil and Human Rights
1629 K Street NW, 10th Floor
Washington, DC 20006
(202) 466-3311
Web site: http://www.civilrights.org

The Leadership Conference on Civil and Human Rights organizes advocacy and lobbying efforts to protect and advance the civil and human rights of all U.S. residents.

National Association for the Advancement of Colored People (NAACP)
4805 Mt. Hope Drive
Baltimore, MD 21215
(877) NAACP-98 (622-2798)
Web site: http://www.naacp.org
The National Association for the Advancement of Colored People works to secure equal rights for all individuals and end discrimination on the basis of race.

National Center for Civil and Human Rights
55 Ivan Allen Jr. Boulevard
Suite 510
Atlanta, GA 30308
(404) 991-6970
http://www.cchrpartnership.org
The National Center for Civil and Human Rights works to educate youth about the ongoing struggle for civil rights and the history of the civil rights movement.

National Civil Rights Museum
450 Mulberry Street
Memphis, TN 38103
(901) 521-9699
Web site: http://civilrightsmuseum.org

Located at the site of the Lorraine Motel in Memphis where Dr. Martin Luther King Jr. was assassinated, the National Civil Rights Museum houses exhibits and collections that increase public knowledge of the civil rights movement and its legacy. It also has research and educational programs.

WEB SITES

Due to the changing nature of Internet links, Rosen Publishing has developed an online list of Web sites related to the subject of this book. This site is updated regularly. Please use this link to access the list:

http://www.rosenlinks.com/CCRM/CRA

FOR FURTHER READING

Adamson, Heather. *The Civil Rights Movement: An Interactive History Adventure*. Mankato, MN: Capstone Press, 2009.

Adelman, Bob. *"I Have a Dream:" A 50th Year Testament to the March That Changed America*. Upper Saddle River, NJ: Pearson Education, 2013.

Armstrong, Thomas, and Natalie Bell. *Autobiography of a Freedom Rider: My Life as a Foot Soldier for Civil Rights*. Deerfield Beach, FL: Health Communications, 2011.

Arsenault, Raymond. *Freedom Riders: 1961 and the Struggle for Racial Justice*. New York, NY: Oxford University Press, 2011.

Branch, Taylor. *The King Years: Historic Moments in the Civil Rights Movement*. New York, NY: Simon & Schuster, 2013.

Brimmer, Larry Dane. *Birmingham Sunday*. Honesdale, PA: Calkins Creek, 2010.

Brinkley, Alan. *John F. Kennedy*. New York, NY: Times Books, 2012.

Freed, Leonard. *This Is the Day: The March on Washington*. Los Angeles, CA: J. Paul Getty Museum, 2013.

Haley, Alex, and Malcolm X. *The Autobiography of Malcolm X*. New York, NY: Ballantine Books, 1965.

Jayznka, Kitson. *Martin Luther King, Jr.* Washington, DC: National Geographic, 2012.

Jeffrey, Gary, and Nick Spender. *Medgar Evers and the NAACP* (Graphic History of the Civil Rights Movement). New York, NY: Gareth Stevens Publishing, 2012.

Jones, William P. *The March on Washington: Jobs, Freedom, and the Forgotten History of Civil Rights*. New York, NY: W. W. Norton, 2013.

King, Martin Luther, Jr. *Strength to Love.* New York, NY: Harper & Row,1963.

Krull, Kathleen. *What Was the March on Washington?* New York, NY: Grosset & Dunlap, 2013.

Levine, Kristin. *The Lions of Little Rock.* New York, NY: Penguin, 2013.

Marable, Manning. *Malcolm X: A Life of Reinvention.* New York, NY: Penguin, 2011.

May, Gary. *Bending Toward Justice: The Voting Rights Act and the Transformation of American Democracy.* New York, NY: Basic Books, 2013.

McDonough, Yona Zeldis. *Who Was Rosa Parks?* New York, NY: Grosset & Dunlap, 2010.

McKinstry, Carolyn Maull. *While the World Watched: A Birmingham Bombing Survivor Comes of Age During the Civil Rights Movement.* Carol Stream, IL: Tyndale House Publishers, 2013.

O'Brien, M. J. *We Shall Not Be Moved: The Jackson Woolworth's Sit-In and the Movement It Inspired.* Jackson, MS: University Press of Mississippi, 2013.

Parks, Rosa. *Rosa Parks: My Story.* New York, NY: Penguin, 1999.

Peters, Charles. *Lyndon B. Johnson.* New York, NY: Times Books, 2010.

Pinkney, Andrea Davis. *Sit-In: How Four Friends Stood Up by Sitting Down.* New York, NY: Little, Brown and Company, 2010.

Sullivan, Patricia. *Lift Every Voice: The NAACP and the Making of the Civil Rights Movement.* New York, NY: New Press, 2010.

Williams, Juan, and Julian Bond. *Eyes on the Prize: America's Civil Rights Years, 1954-1965*. New York, NY: Penguin, 2013.

Williams, Michael Vinson. *Medgar Evers: Mississippi Martyr.* Fayetteville, AR: University of Arkansas Press, 2013.

Younge, Gary. *The Speech: The Story Behind Dr. Martin Luther King Jr.'s Dream*. Chicago, IL: Haymarket Books, 2013.

Dirksen Congressional Center. "Major Features of the Civil Rights Act of 1964." Retrieved June 4, 2013 (http://www.congresslink.org).

Henry Ford Museum. "The Story Behind the Bus." Retrieved July 29, 2013 (http://www.thehenryford.org/exhibits/rosaparks/story.asp).

History Channel. "Civil Rights Act." Retrieved June 4, 2013 (http://www.history.com/topics/civil-rights-act).

History Channel. "Greensboro Sit-In and the Sit-In Movement." Retrieved July 29, 2013 (http://www.history.com/topics/greensboro-sit-in).

History Channel. "Ku Klux Klan." Retrieved June 4, 2013 (http://history.com/topics/ku-klux-klan).

Holmes, Marian Smith. "The Freedom Riders, Then and Now." *Smithsonian Magazine*, February 2009. Retrieved September 10, 2013 (http://www.smithsonianmag.com/history-archaeology/The-Freedom-Riders.html).

John F. Kennedy Presidential Library and Museum. "Civil Rights Movement." Retrieved September 10, 2013 (http://www.jfklibrary.org/JFK/JFK-in-History/Civil-Rights-Movement.aspx).

King Center. "About Dr. King." Retrieved September 10, 2013 (http://www.thekingcenter.org/about-dr-king).

Library of Congress. "15th Amendment to the U.S. Constitution." Retrieved July 29, 2013 (http://www.loc.gov/program/bib/ourdocs/15thamendment.html).

Library of Congress. "14th Amendment to the U.S. Constitution." Retrieved July 29, 2013 (http://www.loc.gov/program/bib/ourdocs/14thamendment.html).

Library of Congress. "13th Amendment to the U.S. Constitution." Retrieved July 29, 2013 (http://www.loc.gov/program/bib/ourdocs/13thamendment.html).

NAACP. "NAACP History: Medgar Evers." Retrieved September 10, 2013 (http://www.naacp.org/pages/naacp-history-medgar-evers).

National Archives. "Teaching with Documents: The Civil Rights Act of 1964 and the Equal Employment Opportunity Commission." Retrieved June 4, 2013 (http://www.archives.gov/education/lessons/civil-rights-act).

National Park Service, Martin Luther King Jr. National Historic Site. "Jim Crow Laws." Retrieved June 4, 2013 (http://www.nps.gov/malu/forteachers/jim_crow_laws.htm).

National Park Service, Sixteenth Street Baptist Church National Historic Site. "Sixteenth Street Baptist Church." Retrieved September 10, 2013 (http://www.nps.gov/nr/travel/civilrights/al11.htm).

NobelPrize.org. "Martin Luther King, Jr.—Biographical." Retrieved September 10, 2013 (http://www.nobelprize.org/nobel_prizes/peace/laureates/1964/king-bio.html).

Scholastic. "Rosa Parks: How I Fought for Civil Rights." Retrieved September 10, 2013 (http://teacher.scholastic.com/rosa/sittingdown.htm).

University of Michigan. "Race, Voting Rights, and Segregation: Techniques of Direct Disenfranchisement, 1880–1965." Retrieved June 4, 2013 (http://www.umich.edu/~lawrace/disenfranchise1.htm).

U.S. Department of Housing and Urban Development. "Fair Housing Laws and Presidential Executive Orders." Retrieved September 10, 2013 (http://portal.hud.gov/hudportal/HUD?src=/program_offices/fair_housing_equal_opp/FHLaws).

U.S. Department of Justice. "The Voting Rights Act of 1965." Retrieved September 10, 2013 (http://www.justice.gov/crt/about/vot/intro/intro_b.php).

U.S. Senate Committee on the Judiciary. "The Civil Rights Act of 1964." Retrieved June 4, 2013 (http://www.judiciary.senate.gov/about/history/CivilRightsAct.cfm).

Wormser, Richard. "The Rise and Fall of Jim Crow: *Plessy v. Ferguson*." PBS.org, 2002. Retrieved June 4, 2013 (http://www.pbs.org/wnet/jimcrow).

INDEX

N

O

P

R

S

T

U

V

W

ABOUT THE AUTHOR

Jennifer Bringle has written several books for young adults on topics ranging from homelessness to reproductive rights. Her writing has also appeared in such publications as *Southern Living*, *USA Today*, and the *Washington Post*, for which she covered the fiftieth anniversary of the Greensboro sit-ins. She lives in Greensboro with her husband and cat.

PHOTO CREDITS

Cover, p. 29 PhotoQuest/Archive Photos/Getty Images; pp. 4, 47 AFP/Getty Images; pp. 8–9 Jack Benton/Archive Photos/Getty Images; p. 12 Marion Post Wolcott/Archive Photos/Getty Images; p. 14 Hulton Archive/Archive Photos/Getty Images; p. 17 Don Cravens/Time & Life Pictures/Getty Images; p. 19 Rolls Press/Popperfoto/Getty Images; pp. 20–21 Bruce Roberts/Photo Researchers/Getty Images; p. 22 Paul Schutzer/Time & Life Pictures/Getty Images; p. 25 CBS Photo Archive/Getty Images; pp. 32–33 Francis Miller/Time & Life Pictures/Getty Images; p. 34 George Tames/Archive Photos/Getty Images; p. 37 Buyenlarge/Archive Photos/Getty Images; p. 39 Three Lions/Hulton Archive/Getty Images; p. 41 Consolidated News Pictures/Hulton Archive/Getty Images; p. 44 Everett Collection/SuperStock; p. 50 Chicago History Museum/Archive Photos/Getty Images; p. 52 Paul Conklin/Time & Life Pictures/Getty Images; p. 55 Lance King/Getty Images; pp. 56–57 Barry Brecheisen/WireImage/Getty Images; p. 59 Rex Features/AP Images; cover and interior background images © iStockphoto.com/Victor Pelaez (U. S. Constitution facsimile), © iStockphoto.com/klikk (American flag).

Designer: Nicole Russo; Editor: Shalini Saxena;
Photo Researcher: Karen Huang